THE POWER OF GRATITUDE

7 steps to a life that's happy, successful and meaningful

Daniel J. Martin

Copyright © 2022 Daniel J. Martin

All rights reserved. The total or partial reproduction of this work through any means or process, including copying and IT processing and the distribution of copies via rent or public lending is strictly prohibited without the prior written consent of the copyright holders under the sanctions established in law.

ISBN 979-8848162738

"Gratitude unlocks the fullness of life. It turns what we have into enough, and more. It turns denial into acceptance, chaos to order, confusion to clarity."

— Melody Beattie

CONTENTS

Understanding gratitude 9

Step 1: Mindfulness 21

Step 2: Your gratitude journal 35

Step 3: Look for opportunities in every challenge 49

Step 4: Stop comparing yourself to others 67

Step 5: Take care of your relationships 85

Step 6: Volunteer 99

Step 7: Combine self-gratitude and self-criticism 115

The next steps 123

Acknowledgements 127

Can you give me a hand? 129

Other books by Daniel J. Martin 131

INTRODUCTION

Understanding gratitude

Have you ever felt so lost that you began to think you must be doing something wrong? You put into practice all the lessons you learned from endless books over the years, but nothing seems to work and the happiness and success you long for seem further and further away. As time goes by, your sense of frustration grows and you start to wonder if you've been tricked. You haven't. It's just that there's something missing, but you haven't yet figured out what.

Take, for example, other books of mine from this collection. In them, you can find such potent tools as the power of goals or self-confidence. All of them truly have the potential to change your life for the better and for good. So, when you finish reading them, you feel that you've finally found that missing piece. But you still need two other essential ingredients: first, acting or putting into practice what you have learned; and second, an additional tool that complements and expands on the others. This is what I call the salt of all the tools: gratitude.

Gratitude has the power to add flavor (or meaning) to all your accomplishments and efforts, which might otherwise seem bland or lacking in meaning. I'm sure that more than once while you were cooking, you forgot to add salt to the food. How did the dish turn out? You probably found that it had lost all its charm, right? Maybe the recipe was otherwise perfectly prepared, but the lack of this "insignificant" ingredient meant you didn't enjoy it the way you should have, and you couldn't help but feel that something was missing from it. Well, this is exactly what happens when you put perfectly valid and powerful tools into practice but you forget to complement them with gratitude.

This is why gratitude is such an essential and indispensable tool or habit in our paths towards full, happy lives. However, it's also the toughest tool to master. On the one hand, many people can't even remember the last time they felt truly thankful. Because I'm not just talking about the simple act of saying "thank you" when someone does something for you. I'm talking about a deeper gratitude: one that comes from the heart and manifests itself in the way we think and act. And, on the other hand – and more serious yet – there are those who have *never* experienced that sensation of true gratitude, so they don't know what it means, much less how it should feel.

I'm not here to judge anyone. As I said, gratitude is a difficult habit to master, especially when we're going through hard times. I speak from experience. As I'm sure you know from my other books, when I was little, the financial situation at home was hard. My parents, like millions of people all over the world, always lived trapped in the rat race. From this position of financial precariousness, practicing gratitude – or even the simple act of considering it – may seem like an impossible feat. Especially for a young child who doesn't have many tools in their life backpack. One of these tools, which I discovered later on in my teenage years and which helped me to put into practice the power of gratitude, is the *law of all or nothing*. According to this law, we cannot be in two mental states at the same time. In other words, we can either choose to complain or to be grateful. It's one or the other, but it's not possible to complain and be grateful **at the same time.**

To give you an example, when we were trapped in the rat race, I could choose to be mad because I couldn't go on vacation like most of my classmates, or I could be grateful because I was at home enjoying spending time with my parents:

something which one of my classmates could never do again, after his parents passed away when he was just nine years old. Can you imagine what that boy would have given just to be in my place?

The truth is that there will always be problems in your life, just as there will always be things to be thankful for. But it's up to you, and you alone, to decide what to focus on: it's that simple.

Don't get me wrong – just because it's simple doesn't mean it's easy. The truth is there are many factors and obstacles that make it difficult to master gratitude and to enjoy its benefits, such as procrastination, an inability to "let go", or an entitlement mentality:

1. Procrastination

Or "I'll do it tomorrow". In order for gratitude to become a habit and occur automatically, you need to practice it every day. When we begin to put things off, we end up not doing many of the things that are truly important to us. So if you really want to incorporate gratitude into your life, start now. Have you stopped yet to think about or note down something to be thankful for since you started this book? What are you waiting for? Do it now!

2. An inability to "let go"

Everyone faces difficult situations at some point during their lives. These situations affect each of us in different ways and can cause "negative" emotions such as anger and sorrow. This is not bad, per se, since every emotion exists for a reason and fulfils a role, but when these emotions stay with us for too long, they take root and become toxic. This makes it almost impossible to apply gratitude, because as you know, positive and negative emotions cannot coexist at the same time.

3. An entitlement mentality

"I deserve" is another factor that makes things difficult for us. In fact, this kind of attitude is contrary to the growth of a grateful spirit. It is, essentially, the opposite of gratitude: the more I feel I deserve something, the less grateful I am for it. We should abandon this mindset and overcome feelings of entitlement. When someone feels they are entitled to something, they have little need to be thankful for it: "I don't need to thank anyone – I deserve this. In fact, these people are lucky to have me around. I'm amazing."

Are you beginning to see why so many people find it hard to incorporate gratitude into their lives?

Fortunately, there are many more benefits to practicing gratitude than there are obstacles to it. Knowing what these benefits are in advance will make it easier for you to stay motivated and not get downhearted along the way. Let me tell you about some of them:

7 scientifically-proved benefits of gratitude

1. Gratitude paves the way for more relationships

Saying "thank you" is not just good manners, according to a study published in the magazine *Nature Human Behaviour* – it can also help you make new friends. The study concluded that being grateful to someone we just met increases our chances of establishing a relationship with that person later on. So, whether it's thanking a stranger for holding the door for you or sending a thank-you card to a colleague who helped you with a project, acknowledging others' contributions can bring you new friends and new opportunities.

2. Gratitude improves your physical health

According to a study published in the magazine *Health Psychology,* thankful people experience less pain and sickness. It's not surprising that grateful people are also more likely to take care of their health. They exercise more often and are more likely to go for check-ups, which undoubtedly contributes to a better quality of life and longevity.

3. Gratitude improves your mental health

Gratitude reduces myriad toxic emotions, from envy and resentment to frustration and regret. Doctor Robert A. Emmons, leader of research into gratitude, has carried out multiple studies into the relationship between gratitude and wellbeing. And, as you can imagine, his research confirms beyond a doubt that gratitude increases happiness and reduces depression.

4. Gratitude improves empathy and reduces levels of aggression

According to a study carried out by the University of Kentucky, grateful people are more likely to behave in a prosocial way, even when others' behavior is less friendly. The participants in the study who scored higher on gratitude scales were less likely to retaliate against others, even when they received negative feedback. In addition, they experienced more sensitivity and empathy towards other people and a reduced desire to seek revenge.

5. Grateful people sleep better

It has been proven that keeping a gratitude journal improves the quantity and quality of your sleep. Don't believe me? Try spending just five minutes writing down some of the things you are thankful for before going to bed. I guarantee the results will surprise you.

6. Gratitude boosts your self-esteem

A study published in the magazine *Sport Psychology* found that gratitude improved the athletes' self-esteem: an essential component of optimal performance. Other research has shown that gratitude reduces social comparisons. Rather than holding resentment towards people with more money or better jobs – which contributes to a reduction in self-esteem – people who are thankful are able to acknowledge and appreciate others' achievements.

7. Gratitude improves your mental strength

For years, research has shown that gratitude not only reduces stress, but also plays an important role in helping to overcome trauma. A 2006 study found that Vietnam War veterans with higher levels of gratitude had a lower incidence of post-traumatic stress. Similarly, a

2003 study found that gratitude contributed to greater resilience following the 9/11 terrorist attacks. Acknowledging that we have things to be thankful for, even in our worst moments, boosts our resilience.

As you can see, practicing gratitude has multiple benefits that affect each and every area of our lives, both physically and mentally, and it is an essential component of your path to a happier, more successful and more meaningful life.

I hope I have shown you its importance and that you have decided to master it and make it a part of you.

If so, all you have to do is commit to reading this book from beginning to end with an open mind and without prejudice, and put into practice the **7 simple steps** that I am going to reveal to you. The rest is up to you.

Deal? Let's get started!

STEP 1

Mindfulness

"Everything is created twice, first in the mind and then in reality."
— Robin Sharma

On this journey towards a life of gratitude, the first thing you must understand is that it begins in your mind. That's why, in order to make the path as smooth as possible, you will begin precisely by focusing on your own thoughts. Ask yourself: what things matter to me most? What do I think about constantly? What makes me feel alive? These kinds of questions form part of what is known as mindfulness.

Mindfulness is the inherent ability of a human being to be present in every moment without overreacting or feeling overwhelmed by external goings-on. This means that both you and I have an innate ability to direct our attention and energy on the present moment. But why do we find it so hard to use this ability?

The world has become a tremendously noisy place. New technology – especially social media – has made it too easy for us to be aware of everything that's happening all over the planet. Ultimately, this diverts our attention away from ourselves and towards everything and everyone else. Compounding this is the fact that being busy at all times seems to have become the fashion, and no one wants to be left behind. Having a packed schedule has a detrimental effect on our minds, and most people lead a significant portion of their life on autopilot.

Mindfulness enables us to turn this autopilot off and focus on the present moment: the here and now.

The connection between mindfulness and gratitude

Mindfulness is not a new concept. You may have been practicing it for years without realizing. The problem is that it's also highly possible that you have been leaving out a fundamental aspect of it: gratitude. To get the best results out of your mindfulness, you need to introduce gratitude into it. This is because, although mindfulness helps you to get out of your head and into the present moment, gratitude is the magic pill that improves your mood and makes these practices more beneficial.

Mindfulness enables you to observe yourself, others and the world without judging and with a sense of curiosity and acceptance. Gratitude helps you to realize that there are many more qualities in you, others and the world that you can be thankful for. Together, these practices feed into what Buddhists call the "Superior Being" within you.

Thanks to mindfulness, not only will you be able to accept things as they come, but you will manage to be grateful for them. It's like having a mental list of all your qualities and being grateful for each of them. Mindfulness is a real game-changer when it comes to gratitude.

In addition, another big advantage of mindfulness is that you can use it to trigger gratitude by using one of its many anchoring exercises.

An anchoring exercise consists of associating a stimulus, which could be visual, olfactory or kinesthetic, with an emotional state. When you repeat the stimulus, you evoke the emotional state you had when you created the anchor.

The origin of the study and the importance of anchoring are attributed to Ivan P. Pavlov, the Russian psychologist and physician who won the Nobel prize for medicine in 1904. For Pavlov, anchoring meant associating a stimulus (ringing a bell) with a physiological response (salivation). This happened due to the behavioral association known as a conditioned reflex.

Subconsciously, we are continually exposed to anchors. For example, you may hear a song and experience a certain emotion due to the music reminding you of something or someone. You may also smell a perfume and immediately be transported to a moment in the past, reliving it.

When you understand this, it is easy to see that you can use this technique to condition yourself to practice gratitude automatically. You can create anchors that remind you to be grateful at all times by applying some basic mindfulness techniques.

Ultimately, your goal is to create a life in which gratitude becomes your new normal.

5 basic mindfulness exercises

1. Deep breathing

One of the most widely-used mindfulness techniques consists of paying attention to your breathing.

Breathing is a cyclic and automatic act that keeps us alive and connected to the present at all times.

We normally breathe without thinking about it, but breathing is the number-one way our body nourishes itself, so being conscious of it and regulating it can give you more self-control.

One breathing exercises you can practice is the following:

a. Lie face-up on a stable, hard surface.
b. Place one hand on your chest at heart level and the other on your abdomen.
c. Close your eyes and begin to inhale through your nose, trying to bring the air down into your belly, feeling it rise.
d. Once your abdomen is full, take the rest of the breath into your chest until you have fully inhaled. Do this slowly, counting the seconds.
e. Hold your breath for two seconds.
f. Begin to exhale slowly through your mouth for the same number of seconds that your "in" breath lasted.
g. Repeat this process for a few minutes.

2. Observe your thoughts

Traditional meditation aims to empty your mind, stopping thoughts of all kinds.

However, this may be an overly ambitious goal in our frenetic western society, so mindfulness aims instead – and it's still no mean feat – to play with our attention, focusing it on something specific and so slowing the swirling of our thoughts and distractions.

For example, you can undertake the above breathing exercise while focusing your attention on the very act of breathing.

While you do this, you will find that dozens of intrusive thoughts appear in your mind, trying to disconnect you from the present moment.

The present moment is simply what is going on while you are breathing. Intrusive thoughts, however, will take you to the past or future. Don't worry – be kind to yourself and try to gently bring your attention back to your breathing.

Do this any time an intrusive thought invades the process.

Our minds are uniquely able to observe themselves, and the more you practice these exercises the better you will understand yourself and be able to control yourself, and the easier this will become.

3. Identify your emotions

I'm sure it's not just thoughts that distract you – usually, thoughts come hand-in-hand with various emotions.

In our everyday lives, we are exposed to many events that cause emotional reactions. Most of us are carrying around a heavy backpack of feelings which we have repressed and masked in order to be able to go about our lives.

We seek distractions and try to stay busy so that we don't have time to think about them. This is why, when we're alone and silent and we let our guards down, those pent-up emotions can emerge and remind us that they are still there.

It's quite common for people to feel discomfort, sadness or even anxiety the first time they practice mindfulness: the very opposite of what we think we should be feeling. This is totally natural; don't let it scare you or discourage you from continuing.

When you clean, you first have to tackle the "trash": the first thing you find when you take away everything you created in order to hide it.

One technique that can help you to deal with these emotions is to observe what they are like and how they feel without trying to repress or get rid of them.

You might also find it useful to give them a name.

When you give something a name, you make it more manageable and less unknown. This will help you to be better able to dominate your emotions rather than being dominated by them.

4. Use visualization

The mental world can be too abstract, and when we are used to a world of sensory stimuli, we can often get lost in it. Using visualization techniques can help us to better manage our thoughts and the feelings that arise from them.

We have a very wide mental range of emotions linked to certain images, objects, colors and so on. The aim of visualization is to connect specific images and thoughts with specific states of mind. Then, all you will have to do is think about activities or places that, for example, give you a pleasant feeling of calm, in order to bring those same sensations into the present moment.

You can also start to generate new associations during meditation, so that when you enter a relaxed state in which you feel at ease, you can internalize it (create an anchor) by associating it with a certain image. This way, with practice, you can return to that same relaxed state simply by visualizing that image.

5. Be aware of your body

Often, our emotions hide behind our body in the form of conditions: muscle tension, skin problems, digestive issues, and so on.

For this reason, when you practice mindfulness, pay very close attention to your body.

A simple way to increase your awareness of your body is to do a simple daily exercise calling body scanning. This consists of a mental exploration of the different areas of your body in sequence, from your head to your toes or vice versa, paying attention to how they feel.

When you do this exercise, you will notice how certain thoughts generate certain physical sensations. Gently use your breathing to calm them down and bring you into that present moment where nothing is more important than the good fortune of being alive.

If these five exercises have piqued your interest but you find them difficult to put into practice, I recommend using an app you can download onto your cellphone. Personally, I use Headspace, one of the most popular meditation apps worldwide. With its free version, you can practice these five exercises in a simple way with the help of an audio guide that will enable you to internalize them and therefore make use of them when you most need to.

Chapter summary

Gratitude, like everything else, originates in our minds – so, if you want to master it, it's logical to begin by focusing on your thoughts. To help you do this, you may find mindfulness a very useful technique.

Mindfulness is a very powerful tool that helps you direct your attention to the here and now. This way, while mindfulness is helping you to turn off that autopilot and focus on the present moment, gratitude can enable you to be thankful for it.

STEP 2

Your gratitude journal

"We can only be said to be alive in those moments when our hearts are conscious of our treasures."
— Thornton Wilder

Have you ever learned or memorized something to perfection only to find, after a few days or weeks, that that knowledge seemed to have disappeared almost completely? Personally, that was my day-to-day (or, rather, my semester to semester) in my student days. I was a model student in a mediocre education system (to put it lightly). That doesn't make me too proud. The "good" thing is that forgetting the abundance of stupid things you might be taught in school can teach you that school or even college are not that important. But what happens when you need to remember something you learned? What if we're talking about truly important things? The answer is very simple: if you want to remember something, write it down.

The human memory is limited. Until recently, it was believed that people could only remember five to seven things at once, but recent studies have shown that we may only be able to remember two or three. With an ever more distracting environment, our short-term memory space is diminishing.

If we can only remember two or three things at once, how can we hope to remember all the things we should be thankful for? To refresh your memory, you need to stimulate it, and one of the most effective, simple and low-cost ways to do this is via a gratitude journal.

A gratitude journal is a diary or notebook people use to reflect and focus on the positives in their lives. It's a very widely-used practice in positive psychology, which has been recognized as effective in improving the lives of millions of people. So, if you have never tried carrying a gratitude journal with you, it's time to start. Can you think of an easier way to improve your life?

But why is the journal thing so important? Why isn't it enough simply to think about the things we have to be thankful for, and save ourselves time writing them down? Well, there are two simple reasons. Firstly, as we have just seen, our memory is limited. And secondly – and even more importantly – our limited memories are selective. This means that we tend to focus on negative memories rather than positive ones.

This phenomenon is known as the negativity bias. According to neuroscientist Rick Hanson, the negativity bias is a consequence of evolution, given that our ancestors learned to make smart decisions based on the risk involved in them. Those humans who better remembered negative events, and thus avoided them, had greater life expectancies.

This pattern was passed down from generation to generation, conditioning the human brain to afford more importance to negative aspects, pay more attention to them and bear in mind potentially dangerous events for the physical, emotional and psychological integrity of the individual.

This means that a phenomenon which, millions of years ago, increased our chances of survival, ended up working against us. If we don't actively do something about it, it will hold us back.

Fortunately, in order to cancel out this evolutionary vestige that burdens our lives, we don't need to undergo any complicated microsurgery or wait another few million years for our brains to realize that this feature no longer aids the survival of the species. All we have to do to counteract this negativity bias is... keep a gratitude journal.

A gratitude journal will help you on the one hand to focus on what you (not your mind) want – good things – and on the other hand to look back on those good things whenever you want and when you decide to. This way, even on your worst days, those when some terrible event spoils everything and it seems impossible to find anything to be grateful for, you can use your diary to remember all the good things in your life and even relive the gratitude and happiness you felt when you wrote them.

5 tips for keeping a gratitude journal

Writing in a gratitude journal is like keeping a personal journal. The only difference is that gratitude journals are much more profound, as they involve a more critical view of your experiences. None of them require a specific format. Since they are such personal notes, you can write them with total freedom and flexibility. This means there is no wrong way to keep a gratitude journal.

However, there are some aspects that are good to bear in mind. Simple indications that make the difference between obtaining the benefits of keeping a gratitude journal, and not:

1. Use a pen and paper

The first thing you should do is ensure you write your journal using a pen (or pencil) and paper.

With all the technology we have just a click away today, you might be tempted to use your computer or download an app (there are lots of them and they can be very good). Don't do this.

When we type, we use a very limited and non-creative area of our brains. However, when we write by hand, using a pen and paper, we involve more of our brains more profoundly. This is because writing by hand means creating each letter separately. One by one. This, of course, requires more skill and intent than typing. It's also a slower way to write, so it leaves a more lasting mark on our minds.

Researchers from the Norwegian Centre for Learning Environment and Behavioural Research in Education also discovered that reading a handwritten text activates more areas of your brain than reading one typed on a computer. This is because our memories are linked to the movements of our hands as we write.

2. Find your motivation

Have you ever begun an activity without having a clear reason why that would help you overcome the difficult moments? How did it go? I'm guessing not great.

Do you know how many people decide to sign up for the gym every year solely because "it's January 1st"? Do you know the percentage of quitters before that month is even up? It's more than 80%! This is because there is no real or important motivation underpinning that action. There is no intent, which is why your brain tells you that you can quit at any time. However, the percentage of quitters among people who sign up for the gym **for a well-defined reason**[1] is drastically lower.

Starting a gratitude journal is just like starting the gym. You need to have real motivation to do

---

[1] If you haven't yet, then I recommend looking over the chapter "clear and realistic aims" from my book *The power of self-confidence*: https://geni.us/psc-book

it: a reason that helps you to overcome obstacles and maintain your new habit even on difficult days.

Luckily, given that a human's ultimate goal is to find happiness and numerous studies have demonstrated that keeping a gratitude journal is one of the simplest and cheapest ways to do that, maintaining this habit is relatively easy. I mean, isn't being happier a sufficiently important reason?

Because if you're not determined to be happy, then keeping a gratitude journal will be of no use to you.

3. Be specific

Being specific will make your journal more authentic and meaningful. Remember that you are writing in your gratitude journal so that you can look back on the positive things in your life.

What good will it do if you don't include specific details that stimulate your memory and help you to relive those happy moments? Instead of writing something like "I'm grateful for my family", try writing "I'm grateful that my mom's test results came back okay", "I'm grateful that my brother got an A in Math", "I'm grateful that my dad's job has given him some time off so we can go fishing". When you go into detail, it will be easier for you to remember the happiness and gratitude you felt at the time.

4. Choose your moment

Some studies suggest that writing in your gratitude journal just before you go to bed can help you sleep better at night. Often, it seems that our heads are waiting to hit the pillow to start going over all the things we didn't do that day or worrying about what we need to do tomorrow. Writing in your journal before you go to sleep can help reduce stress and get you to sleep. On the other hand, you might find that writing in your gratitude journal first thing in the morning helps you start the day off on the right foot or with that extra boost of motivation.

Ultimately, it's about finding the moment that works best for you and being consistent with it.

Personally, I like to write down the things I'm thankful for first thing in the morning and noting down the good things that happened over the course of the day just before I go to bed.

5. Use templates or indications

Great. Now you know how and when you should write in your gratitude journal. All that's left is to know what to write.

To make writing in your journal an easier task that takes no more than five minutes out of your day, you might find it very helpful to use a journal that contains suggestions or pre-written questions to reflect on. This is particularly important at the start, when you're trying to turn this new task into a habit that takes almost no effort on your part.

> **A GIFT FOR YOU:**
>
> If you want to get hold of a copy of the gratitude journal I use to work with my clients, and which has already helped thousands of people in their paths towards a happier and more successful life, write me at *hola@danieljmartin.es* and I'd be happy to send it on to you.

WOULD YOU PREFER A HARD COPY OF YOUR NEW GRATITUDE JOURNAL?

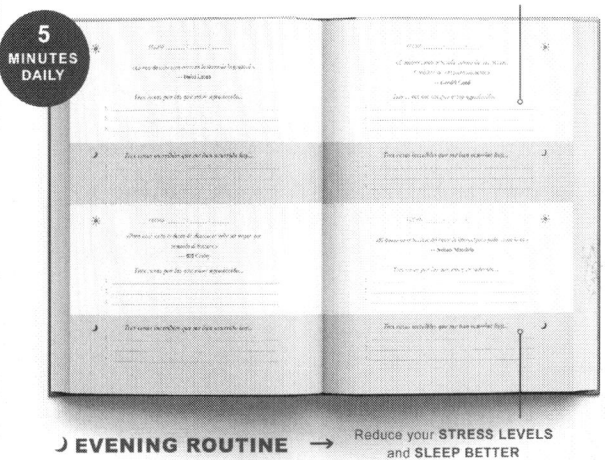

GET IT TODAY ON AMAZON:

Chapter summary

Our minds can't remember everything. To make gratitude more effective, you need to be able to look back on the positive experiences in your life in as much detail as possible. To do this, keeping a handwritten gratitude journal will be essential. Thanks to this journal, not only will you find it easier to remember the things you should be thankful for, but when you write them down, you will make them more concrete and real and prevent the negativity bias that your mind inherited from millions of years ago.

In this way, a gratitude journal will help you to focus on what you want – the good things in your life – rather than what your mind wants, and you will be able to remember them whenever you want just by opening the journal and reading a few of its pages.

STEP 3

Look for opportunities in every challenge

"An optimist sees an opportunity in every calamity; a pessimist sees a calamity in every opportunity."
— Winston Churchill

Whether we want to or not, every day we face many challenges of various kinds. It's inevitable, and we can't control it. We all have our own obstacles that get in the way of success. We need to accept that there will always be challenges in our lives. The question is how we face them. We can do nothing but complain about how unfair the situation is, or we can use it to our favor, looking for the hidden opportunities in every challenge.

All successful people had to face their own challenges at one point. Steve Jobs was fired from his company before coming back later as chief executive and turning Apple into the most sought-after company in the world. Imagine how hard it must be getting fired from your own company. Or Walt Disney himself, who was fired from the local newspaper the Kansas City Star because, according to the editor, "he lacked imagination and had no good ideas". But neither Steve nor Walt let these challenges stop them from achieving success. Quite the opposite. They motivated them to try even harder.

They say that the bigger the challenge, the bigger the success or reward that awaits us.

But the key to letting this happen, to letting our everyday challenges help us to triumph rather than trapping us in a vicious cycle of negativity, is to be thankful. When we complain, we cloud our minds with all kinds of problems. This makes it difficult to gain perspective of the situation, much less to use it to our benefit. Gratitude, on the other hand, clears our minds. It rids us of negative thoughts and shows us the way to the solution. This enables us to gain a better perspective of the challenges we are facing and makes it easier to find the opportunities hiding behind them.

Of course, this is easier said than done. You need a lot of courage, resilience and determination. But there is no doubt that you can do it. And I promise it's worth it. All you need is a little guidance, and that's what I'm here for. In this chapter, I'll show you what you need to achieve this change in mindset and how you can begin to turn your challenges into opportunities.

Start by changing your mindset

Remember, gratitude starts in your mind. I don't mean to sound like a broken record, but it's essential for you to remember that while you're reading this chapter. As such, the first thing you need in order to be able to see the opportunities hiding behind every challenge is to change your mindset.

A change in mindset means you will have to reconfigure or reset your mind. This takes work, as it involves changing one or more aspects of your personality that have been a part of you for a long time. So don't expect it to happen overnight. Don't be hard on yourself if you don't manage it on the first try. The trick is to take things slowly and persevere.

Once you have understood this, what mindset changes do you need to implement?

The first and most obvious is to **change your attitude from pessimistic to optimistic.**

I don't mean become a total dreamer. All you need to do is try to see the good side of things.

Pessimistic people think that when bad things happen, they are forever, and that good things are fleeting. These kinds of people feel powerless to change things.

Optimistic people, on the other hand, believe that bad things come and go. They take responsibility for making good things happen. And they are able to turn a streak of bad luck into an opportunity for growth.

The second change in mindset that you need to put into practice is **switching paralysis for action**.

You need to have the courage to face your fears when it comes to new challenges. These fears are reflected in a wide range of different excuses that we use to stay in our comfort zones. We think, whether consciously or subconsciously, that if we stay still, if we do nothing, then we won't run the risk of failure. And the years go by without doing or trying anything at all, then on our deathbeds we regret all the things we didn't attempt out of fear. A fear that exists only in our minds and which, just like the negativity bias, is simply an evolutionary vestige that has no use in today's world.

Never forget that the only failure is not trying.

Finally, you need to **stop your mind from living in the past or future and focus it on the present**.

Too much of the past (melancholy) limits a person, clipping their wings so they can't fly and clouding their vision in the face of new possibilities. It turns them into a victim of their life, where they are not involved in what occurs in it; things just "happen" to them and "they can't" respond. Too much of the past is just a misspent existence.

On the other hand, some people live with too much future (anxiety) – those who watch the clock for tomorrow and suffer what is not yet "real" today. Too much of the future is just a stubborn desire to bring certainty to the uncertain.

Living in the present (peace) means not only stopping thinking about the past or the future, but also learning to enjoy the here and now, fully conscious of it. When we pay attention to detail, we learn to enjoy every moment, we involve our body and soul in everything we do and we even change our perception of the world around us.

The aim shouldn't be to be in the present moment hoping to be okay. The aim should be to be in the present to discover and understand reality. That understanding of reality is what will make you better and enable you to face life's challenges with more wisdom and serenity.

Challenges are inevitably going to arise in life. You can't do anything about that. What you *can* do is change the mindset with which you choose to face the stumbling blocks that will appear sooner or later: some in the form of small setbacks, others devastating events that can demolish everything. If you want to be prepared, begin changing your mindset today.

How to turn problems into opportunities

Now that you know that in order to make the most of the power of gratitude you need to learn to see the opportunities behind every challenge, let's look at five simple tried-and-tested steps to help you achieve that with minimal effort.

1. Anticipate

One thing about opportunities is that they always appear when you least expect it. This quality alone presents a real challenge, since it tends to leave us with very little room for maneuver. If you want to be ready next time an opportunity presents itself, you need to anticipate it. The best way to do this is to expect problems to crop up. Don't get me wrong – I'm not asking you to be pessimistic. At all. What I mean is that you should expect problems to arise, but with the mindset that you will overcome them.

Another way to be prepared for new opportunities is to think worst-case scenario in advance. What do I mean? I mean that before you start a new project or go for your next goal, brainstorm potential problems that could come up. Think about the worst-case scenarios and write down the best solution to each of them. This will help you stay one step ahead, and when problems come, you'll view them as nothing more than little setbacks.

2. Take meaningful risks

Life is full of risks, and there are countless opportunities hiding behind them. Almost all opportunities carry some risk; the trick is to only take those which are meaningful. I like to use that word because, even when they don't bring us what we had hoped, they teach us important lessons. So don't be afraid to ask for that raise you know you deserve, ask out the guy or girl you like, or start that project you've been considering for so long. Successful people take risks. If you want to be successful too, you need to do the same.

Careful! This is not a call to be irresponsible. Driving at a hundred miles an hour to get to a work meeting with the "excuse" that your promotion depends on it is not a meaningful risk – it's reckless. There is a big difference between making the most of an opportunity and simply being rash. The former will help you to triumph; the latter could have irreparable consequences.

3. View failures as learning opportunities

Charles Dickens said: "Every failure teaches a man something, if he will but learn."

The purpose of failure is to help us grow, learn and get stronger so we can become people deserving of our dreams; in other words, failure is an integral part of success.

Failure is one of the essential steps we must take when walking the path to success. When we try something and it doesn't work out, we have an opportunity to learn and get stronger before we take the next step. Life is about advancing gradually toward our dreams, and part of that journey is acquiring the tools we need to get there.

The next time you feel a sense of failure settling over you, follow these steps:

a. Take responsibility for the things that happen in your life. It's up to you to make them different next time.
b. Don't blame yourself; remember that failure doesn't mean there's something wrong with you, it's just another step on your journey of growth that will lead you to your goals.
c. Think about alternative ways of achieving your aims, define new strategies and draw up a plan for achieving them.
d. Finally, don't be ashamed to ask for help. Sometimes we forget that there are people around us who care about us and are ready to lend a helping hand.

4. Focus on the things you can control, accept the things you can't

"God give me the serenity to accept the things I cannot change, courage to change the things I can, and wisdom to know the difference." – Reinhold Niebuhr.

The Serenity Prayer appears in Buddhist texts from the eighth century, as well as Jewish writings from the eleventh century, although the oldest version is from the Greek Stoic philosopher Epictetus.

Epictetus said that we are responsible for certain things, but that there are others we cannot take responsibility for. If you truly understand the difference between what is and is not within your control, and you act accordingly, you will be psychologically invincible and immune to the rollercoaster of luck.

Of course, this is much easier said than done – but I assure you that it works.

For example, imagine you are preparing your resume for a possible promotion. If your goal is to get that promotion, you could end up being disappointed. There's no guarantee you'll get it, because the outcome is not (entirely) within your control. Although it's true that you can influence it, it also depends on a set of variables outside your reach. That's why your aim should be internal: if you adopt Stoic thinking, you will be able to consciously create the best resume possible, then mentally prepare yourself to accept any outcome with serenity, knowing that sometimes "the universe" works in your favor, and sometimes it doesn't.

So the next time something happens to you that you don't like, ask yourself: can I change it? If the answer is no, try to accept it as soon as possible and carry on with your life; if the answer is yes, take action and change it. In either of these cases, enjoy it.

5. Always look for opportunities

Have you ever noticed that when something new grabs your interest – like that new car you're thinking about buying – you start to see it everywhere? It's not that hundreds of new cars have materialized overnight and been strategically placed around your local area for you to see. Those cars were already there, you simply hadn't noticed because your focus was elsewhere. The same applies to opportunities. This means that if you focus too much on your problems, that's all you'll see. On the flip side, if you're on the lookout for new opportunities, you'll discover that they are all around you. In reality, they were always there – you just weren't prepared to see them.

Chapter summary

We all face a wide range of problems and challenges in our daily lives. However, while some people wallow in them, others use them to their favor. The first group contains people who do nothing other than complain about their situation, as if they had no responsibility for it, and the second group contains people who take responsibility for everything that happens to them and seek the hidden opportunities behind every challenge that life throws up.

Focusing on opportunities rather than problems is another way to make the most of the power of gratitude. This mentality will help you to see the good side of every situation, illuminating the path to reaching your dreams and goals. However, it's not easy. You have to begin by changing your mindset, transforming your pessimistic attitude into an optimistic one and substituting a paralyzing fear of failure for taking action, preventing your mind from living constantly in the past or future so that it can focus on the present.

STEP 4

Stop comparing yourself to others

"Other people's lives seem better than yours because you're comparing their director's cuts with your behind the scenes."

— Evan Rauch

Have you ever felt insignificant when you compared yourself to people around you? Everyone seems so happy and successful that your achievements are nothing in comparison. The funny thing is that, most likely, they're secretly comparing themselves to you too. So you both end up trapped in a game of silent comparison while torturing yourselves thinking about how the other person is better than you. It's one of life's great ironies.

I have learned through experience that your current position, whatever that is, is someone else's dream. They're looking at you and thinking: "if only I had their job, their house, their partner, their hair... everything would be perfect." This fact alone seems to me to be reason enough to reconsider things. But, undoubtedly, the greatest reason to stop comparing yourself to other people is that it makes you miserable and it stops you from appreciating the good things in your life. Remember that nothing is forever. Don't waste the opportunity to be thankful NOW for all the things and people in your life just because you're distracted with silly comparisons. Don't make the mistake of not knowing what you've got till it's gone.

Comparing yourself to others, trying to be someone you're not, is a game you can't win. There is only one you in the universe, and the same is true for everyone else. It's simply not possible, and trying to fight that fact will take its toll on you.

Of course, comparing yourself to others in a healthy way can have its advantages. Seeing that someone else has achieved the goals you're trying to reach but which seem impossible right now can be a great source of motivation. "If they can do it, I can too." Having a model to follow can help you reach your goal sooner, since it gives you a clear path to success which includes the steps you need to take, the focus you should use when applying those steps, and – most importantly – the pitfalls to avoid.

But be very careful. Don't confuse comparing yourself with an example to follow – that person who's taken the path you want to take and who has reached the goals you want for yourself – with comparing yourself to everyone you come across. As I've said, doing this won't benefit you at all. Quite the opposite. It's one of the most toxic and destructive habits there is.

Reasons to stop comparing yourself to others

I'm sure that, without me even saying anything, you can think of a bunch of reasons to stop comparing yourself to others. Perhaps just the low self-esteem and inability to see the good things in life that I mentioned before are two weighty reasons to quit this harmful habit. But, if you're still not totally convinced, here are a few more.

1. We never get the whole picture

Take a look at your social media and you'll see that everyone seems to be living perfect, incredibly glamorous lives. Trips, events, boats, white sandy beaches, bottles of Moët poured over their heads… Well, it's not true. Or at least, it's not the whole truth.

It's totally normal, when sharing something on social media, for us to show the best parts of our lives: the photos where we look the best, not the ones with one eye half-closed, the scarce moments of leisure and fun instead of the forty-something hours holed up working, our accomplishments rather than our mistakes, and so on.

We all show the best versions of ourselves. There's nothing wrong with that. The worrying thing, and the thing you must keep in mind before you compare yourself to anyone else, is that there more and more people are sharing moments that never existed with the sole aim of filling a void within themselves. They invent a parallel reality for their social networks.

Before, only sellers of Herbalife (or whatever other multi-level marketing company) were the ones spending a month's savings on renting a Lamborghini or an oceanside mansion just to take a picture and convince you they're living amazing lives full of luxuries paid for by selling protein shakes. More people do it these days. And it's not because they're selling something – it's just so they can get a handful of likes.

We are experts at window-dressing reality, especially when we don't like the reality we're living in.

As if this weren't enough, remember that we never know what someone else is going through. It may be that, despite appearing successful and ecstatic all the time, their dad is sick in hospital, or they've lost their job, or their partner just left them. So be careful what you wish for when you wish to be someone else, because it's entirely possible that that person would give anything just to be you.

2. It cripples your creativity

When you constantly focus on others, you start to do things like them. You might stop dressing in your own style and start buying the same clothes as that Instagram influencer who looks so good in them, or you might discard a business idea you've been mulling over in favor of investing your savings in Bitcoin because all your friends made a truckload of money doing it.

There are two sad things about this.

The first, as I already mentioned in the above point, is that **you're not getting the whole picture.** Maybe that influencer you follow only wears those clothes because she's been paid to. Maybe your friends who "made a killing with Bitcoin" invested in it a long time ago – when it was actually a good time to do it – or did it with money they could spare rather than taking out a loan like you're thinking about doing, or maybe they only tell you about the rises and forget that, with the falls, they're no better off than they were at the start, or even worse off.

The second is that **it stops your ability to be creative** and analytical. You may have a unique fashion style, but you'll never know because you're trying to be someone else. You might have a groundbreaking business idea, but you park it so you can copy what others do and "play it safe". Sadder still is that someone else could end up developing "your idea" and being successful. And not because they stole your idea – anything you can think of, it will have occurred to someone else first. The difference between those who triumph and those who don't is that the former group carry their ideas out, making use of their creativity and leaving aside stupid comparisons.

If you have been blessed with the gift of creativity, please don't throw it away because of useless self-comparison.

3. It's a waste of time and energy

Comparing yourself is automatic, but that doesn't mean it doesn't take time away from you – the opposite is true. When you start with the comparisons, you think about them over and over, scrutinizing your "flaws" – which are always subjective. You might even search for those same flaws in other people, in the hope that the other person has the same problem, or – even better – that they have it even worse than you.

Whether you're looking up or down at people, comparing yourself just wastes your time. Time you could have spent improving a desirable trait, or simply making the most of it to make your life better.

How much time have you wasted trying to measure up to someone else or to an ideal that was created in order to sell us a product? How much good could you have done with that time? How many people did you neglect to help because of it?

Comparing yourself to others won't get you anywhere, but you lose forever the precious minutes you devote to it. And those minutes become hours, which become days and eventually years.

4. It puts unnecessary pressure on you

Like the mortal you are, I'm sure that right now you have dozens or hundreds of things going on that take up a lot of your time. Maybe you're trying to get a promotion, or even just get a job. Maybe you're battling to give your children the best start in life, maybe you have a sick relative you have to take care of. In short, more than enough things to do to keep you occupied in this life and the next. Why pile more pressure on yourself by adding comparisons into the equation? Trying to be like someone else is like trying to empty the sea with a teaspoon: a task that's as impossible as it is pointless.

Life will take care of keeping you busy with endless challenges to overcome day by day: some nice, some not so nice. Don't be so stubborn as to make your own life even harder.

5. It makes you lose sight of your achievements

Finally, a very important reason to stop comparing yourself to others is that it makes you forget about your own accomplishments. If you don't stop comparing yourself, it doesn't matter what you achieve in life, it will never be enough for you.

At a talk Tony Robbins gave a few years ago in Las Vegas, Tony asked a member of the audience sitting in the front row (seats that cost over five thousand dollars) if he was satisfied with his life. This audience member, who was a well-known American sportsman with a stellar career, a body like an Olympic god and a family straight off the cover of a magazine, surprised the whole auditorium by replying: "No, I'm not satisfied at all."

Everyone, including Tony Robbins, was perplexed.

When he asked the man the specific reasons for this lack of satisfaction, it turned out he had them already perfectly thought out and organized in his head. This famous sportsman was furious because he "only" earned nine million dollars a year when all his teammates made more than ten. Even though he had featured on dozens of magazine covers, he was unhappy with his body because he had 12% body fat, when "ideally" he wanted less than 11%. And, finally, he was frustrated because he had always dreamed of having a big family, and at the age of thirty-seven he only had two kids when his parents had had three boys and two girls.

You're probably thinking this person's not right in the head, am I right?

But remember that that's the same feeling someone has about you when they've been trying to get a job for years and they hear you complaining about yours; when a couple who can't have children see you moaning all the time that your kids aren't as perfect as you'd like; how someone who just lost their mother feels when they have to listen to you complaining that yours calls you every day to ask how you are.

If you can't be grateful for everything you have and for everything you've achieved so far, you will never be able to enjoy the rest of the successes that come into your life.

Steps for a fulfilling life

Now that you know how destructive it can be to compare yourself to others, you need to find a way to kick this bad "habit". The act of comparing ourselves to other people is inevitable, and there's nothing inherently negative about it. Acknowledging that someone else is prettier, smarter or richer than you is not a bad thing. Feeling miserable because of it is. To free yourself from this state of permanent anguish that holds you back and slowly kills you inside, you need a powerful wake-up call. And I can't think of a better reason than **living a fulfilling life**.

The first step to leading a fulfilling life is to understand that it has nothing to do with being rich or famous. As Jim Carrey put it, "I think everybody should get rich and famous... so they can see that it's not the answer." A fulfilling life is defined by your level of happiness and your state of mind. It's that simple. I'm sure you know more than one person who seems to have it all but is still immensely unhappy. In the same way, I bet you could mention someone who has nothing and yet they shine with happiness wherever they go. How do they do it? What steps do you need to take to lead a fulfilling life, too?

1. Find the origin of that comparative behavior

The first step to kicking self-comparison is finding its origin. If you find yourself constantly comparing the same aspects of yourself to other people, it may be that they are the parts of you you're insecure about. You need to find the root cause of this behavior. Do you think you're not tall enough? Not satisfied with your social skills? Work on it. I mean, sure, you can't make yourself taller, but you can cultivate other skills that enable you to get rid of that insecurity.

2. Detox your social media

When it comes to self-comparison, social media has undoubtedly done more harm than good. Firstly, it has created unrealistic standards that many people battle in vain to achieve. Secondly, it has made it even more difficult (TV never helped either) for people to focus on their own lives rather than others'. If you feel that you're in one of these two situations, it's time to detox. You can take the drastic step of going to live off-grid on top of a mountain, opt for a less radical route and have a countryside getaway for a few days, or simply install an app that controls how much time you spend on your favorite social networks.

3. Work on yourself

After detoxing your social media, the next step is to focus on improving yourself. Have you thought yet about how you're going to spend all that time you just earned yourself? What about focusing on improving your personal or professional skills? Don't get ahead of yourself by signing up for salsa classes right away. You've got time. Stop to think about what qualities in yourself you most need to improve. What has the most potential to turn you into the best version of yourself? It may indeed be a physical activity like dancing or the gym that personally gives you most satisfaction and growth. It might be that training in digital marketing will help you get promoted at work. What about making a start on that book you always wanted to write? The possibilities are endless. Choose wisely.

4. Understand that no one is perfect – including you

You should bear in mind that when you take that step and begin to work on yourself, it might not go perfectly on the first try. I'm sure you'll make some mistakes and have slip-ups from time to time; the trick is to remember that nobody's perfect. Every person who has achieved meaningful success in life has made mistakes. Lots of them. I promise you that. So, please, the next time you feel downhearted or blue because you made a mistake, remember: "obstacles are the path".

Chapter summary

There is only one you in the world, and the same is true for everyone else. Comparing yourself to others is a game you can never win; all it does is waste your time and energy, stop you from seeing your own accomplishments, and ultimately completely destroy your self-esteem.

The best antidote to this habit of self-comparison is to lead a full life. To do this, the first thing you need to do is find the origin of this behavior, and the second thing you need to do is shift your focus away from others and onto yourself by working on the qualities that have the most potential to turn you into the best version of you.

STEP 5

Take care of your relationships

"Let us be grateful to people who make us happy; they are the charming gardeners who make our souls blossom."

— Marcel Proust

Research tells us that maintaining good interpersonal relationships is one of the most important elements of our health and happiness. Human beings are social creatures by nature. We are born in a more immature state than any other mammal, which means we need others' help to survive. That doesn't mean we can't be independent, but it's important to understand that you can't do everything by yourself. This is a secret many successful people know and have used to their advantage in order to reap its benefits. It's essential that we cultivate our relationships with other people. There are many ways to do this, but the most relevant is definitely gratitude.

Most people think they only need to be grateful for what they receive from others. On the contrary: we should be grateful for the people we have in our lives. Your current relationships have played a very important part in the person you are today. Think about your life before you met someone who crossed your path, and about how wonderful it is now. You'll realize that it's worth being grateful for.

Gratitude is also an important factor separating a healthy relationship from a toxic one. You should understand that the only relationships worth cultivating are healthy ones. But how can you distinguish between a healthy relationship and a toxic one? The answer is simple. A healthy relationship is full of genuine love, care and respect. When you have a healthy relationship with your friends, family or partner, you will realize that they make you into a better version of yourself. On the other hand, a toxic relationship is full of abuse and a lack of respect dressed up as love This is not the kind of relationship you want to foster.

In other words, one of the keys to practicing gratitude and getting the most out of it is to care for and cultivate the healthy and meaningful relationships in your life. Once you put this into practice, your life will undergo a formidable change.

6 essential elements of a healthy relationship

A healthy relationship can bring great benefits to your life and to that of your partner, friends and family. But achieving a successful relationship is not easy. Fortunately, there are some elements that will help you to sow the seeds of one with those around you.

1. Take responsibility for your own happiness

The first step to creating a healthy relationship is to take charge of your own happiness. Always remember that no one should have so much power over you as to determine whether you are happy or unhappy.

A happy life depends on several factors: your hobbies, your tastes, your activities, what you eat, your dreams, your goals... all of this helps to balance you and make you feel completely satisfied.

Depending entirely on someone else can be a surefire path to unhappiness and emotional disaster. Neither your friends, nor your family, nor your partner should have that much power over you.

2. Establish and respect your boundaries

An emotionally healthy person has boundaries and respects them. When these people enter a healthy relationship, the first thing they do is set down those boundaries and respect them.

Being clear about the boundaries you want others to respect is crucial, since when you let a new relationship affect them, negative emotions such as frustration and despair can arise. That's why it's important to talk to your friends, family and partner so that everyone knows and respects your boundaries, and you do the same for them.

In short, relationships where boundaries are not respected tend to be damaging, exhausting and very painful.

3. Accept and respect disagreements

Thinking that a healthy relationship is completely free from issues, anger or disagreement is a mistake. It's actually quite the opposite. Disagreements are actually totally natural and healthy and will help to evolve and improve all your interpersonal relationships.

We each have our own particularities, so encountering differences with other people is totally normal. As such, if you want to create healthy relationships, you need to learn to respect all beliefs and differences, whether they're about religion, politics, lifestyle or any other topic.

When disagreements arise, what's important is to know whether an argument makes sense and when it's better not to make a big deal out of it.

When you find yourself in a situation that's really worth it, take your time to think about how to resolve it. It's important to start the dialog with an open mind so you can listen to the other person's point of view. Maybe you can't reach an agreement on everything, but you do need to accept and respect the person's ideas.

The most important thing is to avoid trying to force others' opinions to match your own.

4. Compromise

When it comes to interpersonal relationships, remember that you can't control the other person, so compromise is essential. When you reach a compromise with your friends, family or partner, you're offering them your time and attention.

This means that you need to support your loved ones when they need it, and you'll get the same from them.

We all have happy times and other more negative times. That's why it's so important and share with and respect each other. The more you share with your loved ones, the stronger and more solid those relationships will be.

5. Always be honest

Lying is toxic. We all know that. The only way you can achieve a healthy relationship is to force yourself to be honest at all times.

It's true that there are moments when telling the truth is difficult or painful, but in the long-term, it's the right path. When you talk honestly and sincerely with the other person, you foster a bond based on safety and respect.

6. Dedicate time to yourself

In order to have a healthy relationship, it's important that you take some time for yourself: to take care of yourself, listen to yourself, understand yourself. That's why, at least once a week, you should make some time to do something you love or that you're passionate about.

Spending time alone gives you the chance to get to know yourself better. In fact, maintaining a sense of individuality is essential to keeping all your relationships healthy and balanced.

Some people see spending time apart as a sign of unhappiness, but it's not. It's actually a fundamental part of discovering and modeling your identity.

Benefits of healthy relationships

Over the course of our lives, both the quantity and quality of our relationships have a huge impact on our physical and mental wellbeing. We can state without a doubt that good relationships help us to live longer and better.

Would you like to know what **specific benefits** healthy interpersonal relationships can bring you? Here are a few examples:

- They reduce the risk of neurodegenerative disease. People who have regular satisfactory social contact with others are less likely to suffer from dementia or Alzheimer's.
- They reduce stress. Caring about and for others and feeling like part of a group releases hormones that lower stress levels.
- They make us happier. Depression is directly associated with a lack of friends.
- They delay ageing. Social relationships slow down the ageing of cognitive functions by up

to 75%, such as memory, perception speed, visual-spatial capability, etc.
- They make you live longer. Friendships, romantic relationships or simply being connected to someone reduces your risk of dying by 22%.
- They help to resolve problems. Talking to other people helps us to improve our intellectual capacity and be better at resolutions.
- They improve the brain's executive functions. Friendships help the cognitive skills that enable us to anticipate and set goals, make plans and schedules, begin mental activities and carry them out efficiently.
- They prevent obesity. Socialization acts as a food substitute and prevents the overeating that can lead to excess weight.
- They lower your risk of cardiovascular disease. Several studies have confirmed that people with close friendships are up to 85% less likely to suffer from heart disease.

How can you improve your relationships?

Sometimes, we focus so much on our existing relationships that we forget to meet new people. Or, on the flip side, we may be so obsessed with the idea of widening our social circle that we neglect our current friends. It's important to think about the kinds of relationships you want to work on: strengthening your existing friendships or expanding your circle of friends and acquaintances.

In order to reinforce your current relationships, it's usually enough just to call or write them. Social media can be a great help on this occasion. But be careful! It's not enough just to "like" their latest Instagram post. Think about your common interests and suggest a plan that allows you both to share some time together. I'm always available for a coffee or a beer.

On the other hand, if you're looking to meet new people, you could try something as simple as starting a conversation with one of the many people whose paths you cross every day. It could be at work, in class, at the gym. I'm sure you can think of more than one person about whom you've thought "they seem cool". If you're outgoing, it's a done deal.

If you're more of an introvert, like I am, you could always join a group where you share common interests. I recommend the app Meetup. If you don't know it, check it out. It was a real find for me. Just make sure the group you're signing up to isn't trying to sell you anything ;)

As you can see, there are many strategies. All you have to do is pick the one that suits you best. The idea is to share time, experiences and interests with others. Little by little, you'll form a group of people who care about you and who you care about too.

Remember: being happy requires a little effort and dedication. But nothing could be more worth it.

Chapter summary

No man is an island. In order to get ahead in life, we need other people. That's why we have to make sure we cultivate healthy relationships – ones that help us to grow and turn us into a better version of ourselves – and turn away from toxic relationships that only bring us pain and hold us back.

Maintaining a good relationship with those around you does require a little effort and dedication on your part, but the countless benefits for your physical and mental health are one of the best – if not *the* best – investments you could make in yourself, and they guarantee you a longer and more rewarding life.

STEP 6

Volunteer

"The best way to find yourself is to lose yourself in the service of others."

— Mahatma Gandhi

When life is going well, it's easy to start taking things for granted. We start complaining about the slightest frustration and forget to be thankful for the things we have. This sends us into a loop of endless dissatisfaction. Nothing we have or manage to achieve seems like enough. It's not until we lose something or someone we were taking for granted that we wake up from that stupefied state.

But we're not entirely to blame. As we've seen in previous chapters, our brains are wired to focus on negative events over positive ones, and to remember them for longer.

In order to combat that undesirable evolutionary trait, we need some emotional triggers that remind us of the positive things in our lives. Triggers that help you to appreciate how precious something or someone is to you. One of these triggers can be volunteering.

Volunteering means investing your time, energy and resources in improving other people's lives. It helps you to see the world from a new perspective.

When I worked as a volunteer, I realized that my problems were insignificant compared to those of the people I was helping. I was truly humbled and ashamed of having complained about such stupid stuff for so long.

If you're finding it hard to practice gratitude, signing up as a volunteer could be a great starting point.

Things to bear in mind before becoming a volunteer

Volunteering can take on many forms. It simply consists of helping someone else for free for altruistic reasons. However, in order for the impact of your actions to be as meaningful as possible, there are some aspects to bear in mind.

1. Identify the causes that matter to you

Most volunteering groups or organizations tend to focus on the specific causes they want to improve. If they tried to take everything on, they probably wouldn't do much at all. You already know that a jack-of-all-trades is a master of none. This is the same focus that you should adopt, too.

What drives you? Maybe it's your ideas, your values, solidarity, indignation in the face of injustice, the need to do something useful, your love for nature, or your desire to change the world. This exercise will help you determine what you should focus on and to generate more commitment when it comes to causes that are truly important to you.

2. Assess your skills

Once you've chosen a cause, the next thing you need to consider is how your skills and abilities can be of use to the organization you've chosen. Are you good with kids? With older people? Computers? Do you have first aid training? And so on.

Don't just dive in headlong. Stop for a moment to think about how your skills might fit best with your chosen organization – this will make it more likely for your contribution to have real meaning.

3. Determine how much of your time and resources you can invest

Volunteering shouldn't be something you do sporadically, when you feel motivated or when you "find" some time. Volunteering should be a way of life. Just like healthy eating or working out, volunteering requires consistency and discipline. Luckily, just like those things, the more you do it the easier it gets, and the more benefits you reap in return. That's why, before you sign up as a volunteer, you need to think about how much time you'll be able to invest. Drawing up a timetable will help you focus all your attention on the cause you're working for.

If you're going to volunteer, do it with all your heart.

4. Shop around

There are so many organizations who need volunteers like you – you just need to find one you really love. You could start by asking around associations in your neighborhood, or get straight to searching online. There are some really good online platforms that will help a lot on your volunteering journey. Get on Mr. Google and type "I want to volunteer".

5. Evaluate your experiences

After every volunteering session, ask yourself: "What did I learn? How can I do it better next time? What things am I taking with me? What am I thankful for?" Asking yourself these questions will help you to keep growing, and to get the most out of each new experience.

Types of volunteer work

Volunteering is an expression of solidarity that involves committing to an existing need and collective goal. Wherever those needs exist, there will be volunteering organizations that require active, voluntary participation from people in solidarity. The fields they work in vary widely.

There are as many ways to volunteer as there are needs for it. Let's look quickly at the **10 main types of volunteer work** so you can choose the one that best fits with your interests, concerns and skills.

1. Environmental volunteering

With environmental volunteering, you can get directly involved in environmental conservation and raise awareness of the need to protect nature, sustainability and the planet's ecological balance.

2. Community volunteering

Community volunteering will enable you to take part in civic, neighborhood, collective and citizenship movements for the development and cohesion of a community.

3. Cultural volunteering

Through cultural volunteering, you can get involved in a range of projects related to recovering, conserving or promoting cultural and historical identities, fostering creativity and spreading cultural assets and historical heritage.

4. Sports volunteering

Sports volunteering helps social integration among people in a community, and it offers you as the volunteer the chance to work with sports through altruism.

5. Educational volunteering

Educational volunteering will allow you to work in education with children, young people and adults through programs that provide reading support, school reinforcement, literacy, inclusive education, education out of school hours, school community activities, parents' associations, and more.

6. Leisure and free-time volunteering

Leisure and free-time volunteering works in collaboration with entities that develop socio-educational, cultural and sporting activities and even those associated with the environment with the aim of boosting education and community development.

7. Social health volunteering

Social health volunteering aims to improve the quality of life of people affected by disease, support the relatives of sick people, promote blood and organ donation and transplants, participate in home and hospital care, run awareness programs, promote health and healthy habits, and so on.

8. Civil protection volunteering

Civil protection and humanitarian aid volunteering provides help in emergency situations: pandemics, natural disasters, war, coups, accidents and so on. The tasks you could undertake in an emergency context vary widely: basic help and assistance, medical support, psychological help, food delivery, rebuilding of homes, and more.

9. Social volunteering

Social volunteering is one of the most common types. It works very closely with people experiencing social exclusion: people with addictions or disabilities, children, young people, families, immigrants and refugees, recluses and former recluses, ethnic minorities, homeless people, elderly people, and so on. Its main aim is to promote social integration.

10. Equality volunteering

Equal opportunities volunteering aims to achieve equality between men and women as well as for the most deprived demographics.

The surprising benefits of volunteering

Voluntary work can have a great impact on the world and on the people around us, but it's also important to remember that it offers significant benefits for our own physical and mental health.

Practicing kindness and altruism, doing things for other people and making them feel good, has a power we should not underestimate.

These are some of the surprising benefits of volunteering:

1. It connects you with other people

Spending time volunteering helps you make new friends.

Volunteering is a great way to meet new people. It also strengthens your links to your community and broadens your support network, getting you closer to people with common interests and enabling you to undertake fun and rewarding activities with them.

Volunteering also gives you the chance to practice and develop your social skills, even if you are a little shy or reserved, since you will be regularly meeting up with people who share similar goals to you.

2. It reduces the risk of depression and loneliness

A key risk factor for depression is social isolation. Volunteering keeps you in regular contact with other people and helps you to develop a solid support network that will keep sadness at bay when you're going through difficult times.

3. It helps you stay physically healthy

Volunteering is good for your health at any age, but it's particularly beneficial for older people. Studies have shown that people who volunteer have lower mortality rates than those who don't. In addition, volunteering helps to reduce the symptoms of chronic pain or heart disease.

4. It gives you purpose

Having too much time to think, worry and reflect can be bad for your mental health. Volunteering gives you a purpose: something to structure your day and offer you a sense of satisfaction at the end of the week. At the same time, it's a chance to develop new skills and stay physically and mentally active by tackling new challenges.

5. It brings fun and fullness to your life

Volunteering is an easy way to explore your interests and passions in a fun way. In addition, working as a volunteer will help you find meaning in your life and offer you an interesting escape from your everyday routine.

For all these reasons, I believe beyond a shadow of a doubt that it's worth looking for an opportunity where your abilities and skills can flourish and help make the world a better place while simultaneously helping you, too.

Chapter summary

Volunteering simply consists of helping someone else freely and altruistically. But in order for your volunteer work to have the biggest positive impact possible, before signing up to an organization you first need to identify what causes matter to you most, assess your skills and determine how much time and effort you can invest.

Most surprising of all is that, when you volunteer, not only are you helping other people but you are also helping yourself; volunteering offers significant benefits for your physical and mental health, especially when it comes to gratitude.

When you become aware of the things other people have missing from their lives, you begin to appreciate many of the things you had been taking for granted.

STEP 7

Combine self-gratitude and self-criticism

"Self-criticism must be my guide to action, and the first rule for its employment is that in itself it is not a virtue, only a procedure."

— Kingsley Amis

Like everything in life, gratitude requires balance – particularly gratitude towards yourself, or self-gratitude.

Self-gratitude is the pat on the back we give ourselves when we know we've done something right. Being grateful for our successes and for what we achieve is essential, since it helps us to stay motivated and take on new challenges. But we must be careful, since self-gratitude in excess can cause us to focus solely on our achievements and forget to keep improving.

Remember: there's always room for improvement. If you want to stay at the top of your game, you need to find new ways to keep getting better.

When self-gratitude becomes arrogance, we begin to think we have nothing left to learn, or – even worse – that we are better than other people. Dangerous territory it's better not to venture into. It doesn't matter if you've achieved more or gone further than other people – that doesn't mean you can't still learn from them.

If you stop learning, sooner or later your accomplishments will begin to fade until they are nothing more than a distant memory.

Knowing this, how can we keep on practicing gratitude without running the risk of it turning into arrogance and working against us? It's easy. As I said at the beginning of this chapter, it's achieved through moderation. By maintaining a balance. To do this, we will combine self-gratitude with self-criticism.

Practicing self-criticism simply consists of subjecting ourselves to scrutiny. This way, on the one hand, we will be able to identify our mistakes and thus find ways to correct or improve them, and on the other hand, we will be able to remain humble in the knowledge that we still have much to learn.

This is the strategy that successful people use. They acknowledge and give thanks for their achievements and triumphs, but after the victory they get back to work, conscious of the fact there is still room to improve. This helps to keep them motivated while also focusing on continuing to be the best at what they do.

The goal is not to achieve success once, but rather to maintain a successful life.

How to find that balance

We live in a universe in balance. We can see it in everything around us. From the delicate balance that exists between the carbon dioxide produced by plants and which we breathe, to the great centripetal and centrifugal forces that work together to keep the solar system in harmony. A small alteration to these forces would cause us to fall towards the Sun or drift aimlessly through outer space. The same thing occurs with human beings and gratitude. We need balance in order to function, and the best way to achieve this is to find that midway point called moderation.

Unfortunately, most people find it difficult to locate that halfway point and tend towards one extreme or other on the scale. And yes, as we have just seen, too much self-criticism can be just as damaging as too much self-gratitude.

Continually criticizing yourself hurts your self-esteem, stops you from recognizing or enjoying your success, takes you further away from your goals, blocks and paralyzes you, and causes you to develop a failure mindset that will have a negative impact on every outcome. As you can see, finding a midway point is vital.

To make things even worse, it causes you to develop a mentality of failure. Before you even start doing something, you already believe you won't be able to, which undoubtedly affects your result. Luckily, there is a very simple solution that requires almost no effort.

To maintain a balance between self-gratitude and self-criticism, all you have to do is one simple two-step exercise that takes just a few minutes:

- Step 1: Find something to be grateful for in every criticism.
- Step 2: Find something to improve in everything you are grateful for.

It's that easy.

This is something which, over time, I have integrated into part of myself and which I now do without even thinking about it. Take my books, for example. It's undeniable that writing a book is a great achievement. Even so, every time I finish writing one, I ask myself: what could I do better? How can I improve for the next time? How can I bring more value to my readers? Similarly, when I receive a bad review – something that affects many authors to the point they even stop writing – I immediately look for the bright side, such as the fact that a negative review means I am selling books, when many authors can't say this (on average, you get one review for every two hundred books sold), or that, thanks to that critique, I can correct my book or improve the next one.

But until this technique is a part of you and you do it automatically, the best way to apply it is through your gratitude journal. Seek and write down aspects to be thankful for in all your mistakes, and ways to improve on all your successes and accomplishments.

Make sure there is balance between the things you criticize and the things you're grateful for, and remember: **there is only virtue in the midway point**.

Chapter summary

Self-gratitude and self-criticism are two sides of the same coin. While self-gratitude helps keep you motivated, appreciate your achievements and face new challenges, self-criticism helps you identify your mistakes and find ways to correct or improve them. However, both factors, when taken to the extreme, become a problem. That's why you need to find a halfway point between them.

Moderation is the key to obtaining the best results. And the best way to achieve that is to find something to be thankful for in every criticism and something to improve on in everything you're grateful for. This simple exercise will help you maintain that essential balance for a happy and successful life.

The next steps

Firstly, I want to congratulate you for coming this far. Many people shout from the rooftops that they want to be happier, but do nothing to achieve it. The day you decided to buy this book, you already set yourself apart from the rest by taking that first step toward a more successful and meaningful life.

So... WELL DONE!

And now what?

The next step is simple: **it's time to put into practice what you learned** in this book.

"The world is divided into three kinds of people: a very small group that makes things happen; a somewhat larger group that watches things happen; and a great multitude that never knows what has happened." – Nicholas Murray Butler.

When you read this book, you stopped belonging to the class of people who don't even know what's happening. But be careful; it's easy to fall into the category of those who simply watch things going on. This happens when you know what you need to do, but you never apply it. It's like having the keys to a castle, then trying to headbutt the door down instead of using them.

Similarly, if you want a happier and more meaningful life, you can't stick to theory: you need to put into practice the seven steps you learned in this book. These will be your passport on your journey of gratitude.

You don't need to apply all the steps at once tomorrow. Take things slowly. Read this book again. Choose a step and begin to apply it gradually in your daily life.

When you have internalized this new habit, move onto the next one; don't rush yourself. Remember that each of these habits on its own has the power to change your life.

Enjoy the journey, my friend, and remember:

"It's gratitude that makes us happy, not happiness that makes us grateful."

Hugs to you!
Daniel

Acknowledgements

Of course, in a book about gratitude, I couldn't forget to say a few thank yous.

And there is nothing in this world I'm more thankful for than having my parents, Isabel and Juan, in my life, as well as my girlfriend Kathy and our rabbit, Snoopy.

And naturally, to you, my reader and friend, from the bottom of my heart: THANK YOU.

Can you give me a hand?

As I'm an independent author, your opinion is so important to me and to future readers like you. I would be hugely grateful if you would leave me an **Amazon review** to tell me what you thought of my book **so that I can keep on improving it**:

- What did you like best?
- Is there anything you felt was missing
- Who would you recommend it to?
- ...

Scan and leave a review

Other books by Daniel J. Martin

www.danieljmartin.es/books

Printed in Great Britain
by Amazon